LIVING

Tip

Wondering where to start to keep your living space clean and neat?

Having doubts about food shopping and cooking healthy meals?

Want to stretch your budget and make your money last longer?

No one starts life with an instruction manual; but young people throughout the ages have found that more experienced people can help them learn the skills they need to succeed.

WE WANT TO HELP

In the spirit of passing on wisdom learned the hard way, a community-minded group of men and women have combined their living experiences into this hopefully handy booklet of hints and tips.

Go Ahead,

Read On...

you may be surprised at what you can do!

We would like to acknowledge the support and assistance of all those who have contributed to the making of this booklet. It is our shared hope that this information will help others make the transition to independent living more easily and successfully.

Special thanks go to the ECW and others at St. Francis Episcopal Church in Fair Oaks. Individuals are too numerous to name here, but their accumulated wisdom is evident on every page.

Many thanks to you all—
you know who you are!

This booklet was conceived, created, and edited by co-authors Linda Banta and Kathy Sheehan.

Copyright @ 2008 by Banshee Books

Second Edition 2009

All rights reserved.

ISBN: 978-0-615-25605-4

Nova Art Explosion Clip-Art Copyright @2004

TABLE OF CONTENTS

LIVING ON YOUR OWN:
TIPS AND TRICKS

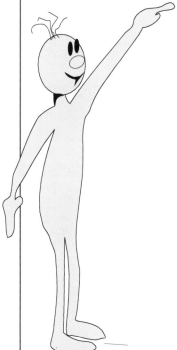

First things first.

MONEY BUDGETING

Take a piece of paper and list all of your **monthly bills,** including expenses such as rent, utilities, child care, gas for your car, car payment, insurance payments, medical insurance, groceries, phone (cell phone and/or home phone), television service, any loans to be paid, and how much money you spend on miscellaneous things such as buying coffee or soda, going to a movie, renting video games, getting your hair cut, or having your nails done. Don't leave anything out.

If you are not sure how much money you spend on everything, carry a pad and pencil with you for a week and jot down anything and everything you spend money on, even if it is just a pack of gum.

Once you know how much money you are spending, look to see if there is any place you can make changes.

- Make do with a cheaper phone service.

- Don't get an expensive television/cable plan. If you need to, just get the **basics**.

- Rent movies rather than going out to shows.

> Think about the difference between "wanting" something and "needing" something.

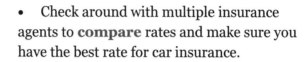

- Check around with multiple insurance agents to **compare** rates and make sure you have the best rate for car insurance.

- Make your coffee at home rather than spend $$$ at a coffee shop.

- Do your own nails.

- Take lunches from home instead of buying fast food.

Save money by learning to cook for yourself!

Once you have your expenses down to their least amount, you can figure out how much you need to earn each week to make enough to pay those expenses and save money too.

SAVING MONEY

Start financial independence by **choosing a bank**. A bank in your neighborhood or near your job would be best.

You will probably need **three** accounts:

SAVINGS ACCOUNT

CHECKING ACCOUNT

CREDIT ACCOUNT

A savings account is your future....

So always pay yourself first.

Get in the habit of putting money in your account from each and every paycheck.

Just think how easily you spend five dollars on a coffee drink. Why not put that five dollars into your future instead? You will be surprised how quickly it grows and how good it feels.

Keep a change jar handy at home and throw in your loose change at the end of each day. It adds up fast.

A **checking account** helps you keep track of your money.

If possible, get the kind of checkbook that keeps a **copy** in the book for you to refer to when necessary.

Write in your checkbook ledger (where you keep a list of the checks you write or your ATM transactions) with **pencil** so that if you mess up in adding or subtracting, you will be able to correct your mistake.

Someone at your bank will gladly show you how to balance your checkbook. Just ask.

When you get your **monthly statement, compare** it to your register-list so you can keep track of how much money you have in your account.

CAUTION: If you use an ATM card, enter the transaction immediately into your checkbook! The one big downfall for checking account users is not entering all their transactions, which results in them thinking they have money in the account that has already been spent.

Overdrawn accounts get penalized by fees and can result in bad credit.

Credit accounts that are consistently paid on time build a good credit history and open possibilities for the future when you might want to buy a car or some other large purchase.

BUT credit accounts that are **not** paid on time, or not paid at all, can haunt you for years.

There are three main credit bureaus: Equifax, Experian and Transunion, who keep track of everyone's credit records.

Credit card companies use these records to decide who is a good risk to loan money to— and who is not a good risk.

Keep your receipts! Invest in some file folders to hold them. Check your bills when they come in to make sure you are not charged for something you did not buy.

Some advice on establishing credit:

*Open an account with your local bank (check to see what the interest fees are). Request a **low spending limit** ($500). This way, you will not be able to owe more than that amount.

*Do not buy anything on this account that you cannot pay off within a month or two. If you **pay a credit card off immediately**, you are not paying high interest fees.

*Do **not** have **multiple** credit cards. It is too easy to end up with more debt than you can pay.

*If you do not trust yourself with a credit card, **do not carry it** with you. Keep it in a safe place at home so that you have it for emergencies but are not tempted by spur of the moment purchases.

*Guard your credit card carefully. Do not let others use it. Do not leave it out where others can see the number. Do not repeat the number out loud where strangers can hear it.

Treat a credit card like real money...it is!!

FINDING YOUR NEW HOME

You can find apartments through the newspapers,

  websites such as *Craigslist.com*,

   in free papers like the *Pennysaver*,

  through services and agencies, or

    through word-of-mouth.

  Be very careful in your choice.

DO YOUR HOMEWORK BEFORE YOU RENT:

Check the ads for a few months ahead so you can compare the rents and get a sense of what the area's average rentals cost.

Check different neighborhoods: What do the people seem like? Is there a lot of trash around the houses or is it neat? Is the area quiet or busy? Visit areas that you think look good, at different times of day and evening. Some places may be great during the day but then have a bad element show up at night.

THINGS TO CONSIDER:

◊If you use an agency or rental service: Will you have to pay a fee? Do they check out the apartment and its owner for you?

  ◊Is the neighborhood safe? Is it near stores; is it near your job? Is it near something that is noisy like a factory or highway?

◇Is the apartment big enough or is it too big? You want enough room without having to pay more in heating or cooling bills. Remember that tall ceilings may look great, but heat rises so your winter heating bills may be high.

◇Is it clean? Pay special attention to the kitchen area and any carpeted areas. Look for signs of bugs or odors.

◇Does the rent include heat, hot water, electricity, air conditioning? Does the apartment have a washer and dryer in it or a laundromat nearby?

◇Is there parking available, if you have a car? If not, is it near a bus line or mass transit?

◇Will the owner want you to sign a lease? A lease generally means you are liable for the rent for twelve consecutive months even if you move; but it also means that you cannot be asked to move before your lease is up. Renting by the month means less security for both you and your landlord.

It is important to carefully read

EVERYTHING
BEFORE you sign anything.

Ask questions if you are not sure what it means.

Do not let someone brush your questions aside.

Have someone you trust read the contract too.

PLANNING YOUR MOVE

Even if you don't have a lot of things to move, it is good to have a plan.

Trick: A good place to get moving boxes is from a liquor store, but do not wait until the day of the move. Stores often break them apart as they unpack them but will save them for you if you ask ahead.

Boxes from a grocery store may carry bugs or smells that you don't want in your home.

Mostly you will need medium sized boxes. If they are too big, they will be too heavy to carry.

Pack your things together according to what room they belong (like kitchen things or bedroom things) and then use a **marker** to write the room on the side of the box so you'll know where to put it as you bring it in. You can also mark boxes for storage or for immediate use.

Arrange ahead for someone to help you move, especially if you don't have your own transportation.

Offer to **swap help** with something else to a friend who has a truck or car to use. Offer gas money too.

Check on your utilities (if you need to turn them on and how much they cost a month).

Get mailing address change packets at the post office. They have change-of-address forms and other information in them.

Tip: It is a good idea, and easier, to clean the apartment **before** you bring your things in.

TOOLS

Many of us, both men and women, agree that one of the best gifts we ever gave ourselves when we set up housekeeping was a tool box. These are tools that you will need right from the very beginning and can be purchased at most stores for a reasonable cost:

• claw hammer (one end is for pounding nails in; the claw end pulls nails out)

• set of screwdrivers (large and small screwdrivers) in both flat head style and what is called a Phillip's head (which looks a bit like a four-sided star)

• measuring tape (get one in a metal case that retracts on its own)

• razor knife that has a retractable blade (comes with extra blades)

• Pliers and adjustable wrench

• box of assorted nails and a box of assorted screws

• spirit level (helps you make things level)

- flashlight (for those places that are hard to see even in the day like under a couch or behind a dresser)

- tape / black electrical tape and regular masking tape

- toilet plunger

- These are not all the tools you will ever need (and certainly the list doesn't include tools for working on cars), but these will help you cope with most emergencies you may run into.

FIRST AID KIT

 As you are moving in, accidents can happen.

Be prepared from the beginning. A small first aid kit can be assembled cheaply and kept in something as simple as a shoebox. Include things like:

3% hydrogen peroxide for cleaning out cuts

Antibiotic cream

Bandaids in various shapes and sizes

Tweezers for taking out splinters

Meat tenderizer—mix with water into a paste/put on bee stings (it really helps!)

An **antihistamine**—such as Benadryl to take after being bitten by any stinging insect

Muscle rub such as "Icy-Hot" for those sore muscles

Aspirin or ibuprofen or acetaminophen

Pepto Bismol

Heating pad

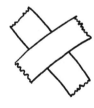

Ice packs—in a pinch, put ice in a zip-lock bag

Buy generic brands and save $$$

KEEPING HEALTHY

When do you need to go to the doctor?

Judith, a registered nurse, has these suggestions for you:

See a doctor if you have:

- *persistent pain unrelieved by two days of over the counter medications;*

- *any loss of sight, movement, bladder or bowel control;*

- *unexplained weight loss; or*

- *unusual or unexpected bleeding.*

Illness **prevention** can be helped by:

- **washing hands** frequently, especially after toileting or coming into contact with someone with a cold or flu;

- following the government **food pyramid** for healthy eating;

- **exercise** for 30 minutes at least 3 times a week; and

- maintain a routine **sleep** pattern.

Emergency First Aid:

- **With any skin break, wash the area immediately with soap and water, rinse with peroxide, and apply a bandaid.**

- **Sprains or strains: use I.C.E. (ice, compression, elevation)**

- **Muscle aches: use moist heat.**

Tips on Health Insurance:

- Apply for entry level jobs with large corporations; health benefits included are usually comprehensive and low cost.

- Check in your phone book for a county operated medical clinic. In the Sacramento, CA area: contact County Medically Indigent Services Program (CMISP) by calling one of the following:

4600 Broadway	874-9670
3950 Research Dr.	648-0970
7171 Bowling Dr.	875-0802
1500 C Street	874-5302

****

BUYING FURNITURE
AND HOUSEHOLD GOODS

What you need to buy will depend on the size of your new home, of course, but there are some "**must haves**":

*a good **bed** and an **alarm clock** with back-up batteries

*a comfortable **chair and a lamp**

*a **table** and chairs for eating and for using as a desk

***dishes** / **glasses** / **pots and pans** / **silverware**

* plastic storage **containers**

*a **toaster** or toaster-oven

***sheets** / pillow cases / pillows / **blankets**

*bath **towels** / dish towels

Thrift stores can be a great place to find usable items—and a few treasures—for your new home.

*Check the phone book for stores near you and then call to see if they have furniture and appliances. Also ask for their sale dates. Most stores have certain days when items are marked way down. Get there early to get the best choices.

*Always plug in electrical appliances to make sure they work, and never buy anything with a frayed cord. You might get a fire when you least expect it.

*Wash any fabric items before you use them. With upholstered furniture, use a spray-on cleaner as soon as you bring the item home.

*Keep in mind with wooden items that a little paint can go a long way in making something usable.

Your most important purchase is your bed.

If you don't sleep well, you can't do your best during the day. Try to buy a new mattress if at all possible.

There are places that sell new mattresses that have slight imperfections or are floor models.

You may need to spend a bit more for a new mattress, but if you can do it, it will be worth the cost.

> ### CAUTION
>
> **Used** mattresses may have bedbugs, and you won't sleep well if you're getting bitten all night.

You may also check stores that supply furniture for displays such as in model homes. Cort is one such store in Sacramento. These stores sell furniture that has been used very little and can be a great savings.

Another option is **yard sales**.
The Pennysaver offers lists of yard sales as well as items for sale, but you can also find many sales just by driving around.

Choose nice looking neighborhoods (where the people probably have bought quality things to start with) but not too rich (you may not find many yard sales in those areas).

Yard sales usually start on Fridays. Plan to go out yard sale shopping early. In these situations, the early bird gets the best pick—but also hit the sales late in the day. People may take less money if they think they're not going to sell the item at all.

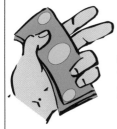

Trick: Always have cash on hand in small bills. Make an offer, preferably with the amount you are offering in your hand so the seller can see it.

Churches may have furniture available for free or for low cost. Or they may be able to help connect you with someone who has items they would like to see go to good use. There are often rummage sales at churches and community centers as well.

DECORATING ON A BUDGET

Things to keep in mind when decorating:

*Sturdy cardboard boxes or plastic boxes can become nightstands or living room tables by putting a tablecloth or cut up sheet over them.

Caution: Do not use cardboard boxes that have had food stored in them. They may have insects nesting inside the cardboard that you can't see.

***Sheets** bought in thrift stores can be made into **curtains, tablecloths, couch covers and more**. Just make sure you wash them first.

***Dollar stores** are great places to find things like dishes, silverware, and pots and pans as well as things to decorate the home.

Keeping your home cheerful will help you stay cheerful too.

*__Paint__ can liven up an apartment or house with small expense and a little effort. Just make sure that your landlord gives the okay for any painting in your apartment <u>before</u> you start.

Trick: If wall-to-wall carpeting has marks or wear spots that won't come out, look for a nice throw rug or rug remnant that might cover up the spot and add color to your room.

Plants or flowers can help make any place feel more like home.

FOOD

STOCKING

YOUR

KITCHEN

There are certain foods that you will find helpful to have in your kitchen. Some are extras; some are basics that you need to have on hand all the time; others will help you make a meal quick when you need to.

Our suggestions include:

Flour

Salt & pepper

Sugar

Ketchup

Mayo

Mustard

Tea, coffee, milk

Margarine or butter

Baking soda and baking powder

Vinegar

Garlic & onion

Crackers

Cereal

Peanut butter & jelly

Bread / tortillas

Oatmeal

Vegetable oil

Spaghetti sauce

Spaghetti / rice / noodles

Various canned fruits and veggies—especially beans (baked, pinto, green)

Canned diced tomatoes

Canned tuna and/or chicken

Canned soups –especially tomato & cream of chicken,

Apples

Cake mix

Pancake mix & syrup

Hamburger and/or crab meat in freezer

Frozen orange juice

Frozen veggies – especially green peas

Tip: Whatever the food, if it is in your cupboard too long, replace it. If you can't remember buying it at all, it may have been there too long. Food that has gone bad can make you sick.

NUTRITION

With Americans fighting an epidemic of obesity and weight-related diseases, you need to be conscious of your food choices.

You are what you eat.

Your car won't run if you put sugar in the gas tank; be just as careful about what kind of fuel you give your body.

- **Eating at home** and taking your lunch to work allows you to make better food choices for yourself. Fast food and restaurant food in general has more fat and salt than you would add at home. Fat and salt makes food tasty, and taste sells, but both can be bad for your health.

- **Do not** overindulge in **caffeine** drinks.

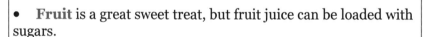

- Read **labels** when you shop. Labels will tell you the nutritional content as well as calories, sugar, salt and fat content.

- Do not let labels fool you. Something may call itself "light" but **read the label** and see exactly what they mean by that.

- **Fruit** is a great sweet treat, but fruit juice can be loaded with sugars.

If you are concerned about being overweight:

Drink more water; eat fresh vegetables; watch out for the additions to salads (dressings, cheese, nuts, etc. add calories, fat and salt); keep cut-up celery, carrots, etc. on-hand to munch on.

Consider joining weight-watchers.

Trick: Don't drink your calories.

Soda and juices can be loaded with sugar and calories or chemicals. Choose water instead.

Walk!

Park a block away from work and walk. Walk around the block a few times at lunch. Walking helps lower blood pressure, helps you lose weight, increases alertness and productivity.

FOOD SHOPPING AND COUPONS

Trick: Never go food shopping if you are hungry. You are much more likely to buy things to eat that are not good for you or are not on your list or are too expensive or you may buy more than you need.

*The Sunday paper is usually a good investment because it has coupons.

Warning: Coupon usage can be hazardous to your financial health if not used carefully. You may buy things just because you have a coupon...and some brands are still more expensive even with money off.

*Only use coupons that are for things you were going to buy anyway. Do not buy something just because you have a coupon for it.

*Check the fine print. Do you have to buy more than one thing to get the discount?

*Compare prices; sometimes the store brand item is cheaper than a name brand item that has a coupon.

*Keep coupons in a separate envelope or plastic container. **Sort through them** and get rid of out-dated ones .

Tip: Make a **grocery list** <u>before</u> you go shopping, and stick to it.

Mary M. says she always shops with a hand-held calculator to keep track of her total so she won't get surprised at the register.

*Buy **seasonal fruits and vegetables**. They will be the cheapest and best.

*Shop at the dollar stores or Walmarts or Long's for **canned and boxed goods.** Other good-price stores are FoodSmart and WinCo.

*Buy ahead on things you use on a regular basis when you see them on sale, like beans or soup or toilet paper.

Fred wrote: *Joining a members-only store may not be worth it for you because you have to pay a yearly fee and need to buy in bulk. But if you do buy food in large quantities, package it into freezer wrapping as soon as you get home and mark each package with the contents and date purchased. Rotate new things to the back of the freezer to use the newest ones first.*

*Use cloth bags for groceries instead of plastic or paper: not only is it better for the environment, but most stores will give you 5¢ a bag credit. They pay you!

COOKING

Cooking for yourself might seem a bit scary...or maybe it is something you just have never done for yourself.

But don't worry... you are not alone!!

We're here to help you!

Let's start with some of the things you need to know ...

Microwave Ovens

Microwave ovens are great for reheating leftovers or defrosting food, but there are a few things to keep in mind:

Do's:

Always use less time rather than more – if food is microwaved too long, it gets rubbery.

Always use microwave safe dishes. Others can crack or break, or they can get too hot and burn you and your food. Microwave safe dishes should be marked on the bottom.

Always cover your food. Waxed paper helps keep moist food moist; paper towels help keep splatter in check.

When you reheat a hot drink or soup, always stir it before taking a sip. Heat can build up inside the liquid and bubble over once disturbed. It's better to do that with a spoon than your mouth.

Vegetables keep their color, flavor and nutritional value better when microwaved rather than boiled.

When microwaving bread or rolls, use the least time, and eat immediately. Bread products get tough when they cool after microwaving.

Potatoes are cooked more quickly if done partly in the microwave before you finish cooking them in the oven or on a grill.

When cooking things like oatmeal or scrambled eggs or puddings make sure you have a large enough dish. They expand as they cook, just as rice does.

Although microwaves are great for heating up a plate of leftovers, microwaves won't make things crispy. But check out toaster ovens a couple of pages ahead. They will.

Clean the inside of the microwave on a regular basis using a damp sponge. Wipe up splatters right away, and they won't be so hard to get off later.

Trick: If your microwave is dirty, fill a microwave safe bowl with 1-2 cups water (add a little lemon juice if you want for a nice smell). Set it in the center of the microwave oven and turn it on to high for 2-3 minutes (you want it to boil and make steam in the oven). Remove the bowl and wipe down the insides with a clean cloth or paper towels.

DON'Ts:

Do NOT cook **eggs in their shells** in a microwave. Eggs can be cooked in microwaves, but make sure you use a microwave safe dish that has been oiled.

DO NOT attempt to bake **tube rolls, muffins or cookies** in the microwave unless they are made specifically for microwaving.

Do NOT put foil or any kind of **metal** in the microwave oven (even dishes with gold or silver trim). They will spark and can start fires.

Just For Fun:

* Quick dessert: Cut an apple in half and remove the core; put in a microwavable dish; fill the center of the apple with brown sugar and cinnamon and raisins; cook for two to three minutes.

*Heat a marshmallow in the microwave and watch it expand – it's good for making s'mores. Just remember to eat it right away before it gets cool...and tough, like bread does.

Toaster Ovens

Toaster ovens are another option that are extremely convenient.

These ovens sit on the counter top and are slightly larger than a regular toaster.

Toaster ovens can make toast, warm food up, even bake potatoes with less power than an oven, equaling less heat and less cost. It also makes things crispy which a microwave oven cannot do.

Stovetops

Use the stovetop whenever you want to **brown** food, such as ground meat; to **fry** something, such as eggs; or to **refry** things like beans.

Use the stovetop whenever you have a **large quantity** of food to cook, such as a pot of soup or spaghetti.

Frying is done in a frying pan with oil. Be careful not to use too much oil or it might spill over and burn you or start a fire.

Tip: To put out a **fire** on a stovetop, **put a lid on the pan** to put out the flame or **pour baking soda** on it.

Do not pour water on fire. Do not try to slap it out with an oven mitt or towel. Do not try to carry the pan to the sink or the door.

Stove's Oven

Ovens provide a dry heat and should always be preheated, which means it should be brought up to the temperature you set it for before the food is put in the oven. Most ovens will make a "ding" when they have reached the temperature set, but with some, like with gas ovens, you can tell the temperature has been reached when the flame goes down.

Ovens are used to **bake** things like cookies, cakes, or bread.

Broiling is done either on the top rack of the oven or in a special compartment under the oven. Keep the door open while broiling anything and watch the food closely so that it doesn't burn or catch on fire.

Ovens also **roast** meats (like roast beef or pork) and poultry

(like turkey or chicken). Roasting means to cook (usually uncovered) in a shallow pan in the oven. The pan must be deep enough to hold any juices that accumulate during the roasting.

Slow Cookers

Slow cookers, otherwise known as **crock pots,** can be especially handy for working families. Ingredients can be placed in the pot in the morning and allowed to cook slowly all day. When you get home, your meal will be ready to eat. **Be careful to set up the slow cooker in a safe place, not touching anything else.** Follow recipes for amounts and times.

RECIPES

Tip: A good **basic** cook book is a good investment for anyone. Check with thrift stores.

GREAT "QUICK "MEALS:

Scrambled eggs or an omelet: add any leftover meat / top with cheese / may be rolled up in tortillas with salsa.

Break eggs one at a time into a small dish (this is so if one is "bad," it won't spoil the others. Add a few drops of water or milk and scramble up with a fork or whisk. Melt some butter or olive oil in a frying pan over medium/high heat. Add egg mixture and stir with a spatula or wooden spoon until firm.

Omelets start with the same mixture of eggs, but when you add them to the frying pan, instead of stirring them up, you scrape all sides to the center as it cooks. While it is still soft, you add cheese or chopped up meat, etc, and fold one side over. Reduce the heat and finish cooking on one side until slightly brown, then flip it over and cook the other side.

Hard Boiled Eggs: Place eggs in saucepan, cover with cold water, add shake of salt, bring water to boiling. Remove from heat and cover . After 15 minutes, empty hot water and put the eggs in cold water until cool.

Toasted cheese sandwiches and canned tomato soup:

English muffins topped with cheese (and maybe sliced tomato) and browned in broiler. Eat with any canned soup.

Baked macaroni and cheese

Cook large elbow macaroni and drain, then make two layers of macaroni with shredded cheese in between and on top in a greased pan. Pour milk over the top until you can just see it through the macaroni; bake at 350 degrees in the oven for about 30 minutes or until cheese is all melted. Nice served with a can of stewed tomatoes heated up.

Pancakes

Make from a mix; serve with syrup.

Tip: Do not use a box of pancake mix or Bisquick that has been in your pantry for too long (like a year). Eating it may make you sick.

Boxed Ramen noodles. (These often have a lot of salt in them so don't eat them too often.)

Peas and Crab Meat

Sautee (lightly fry) peas and imitation crab meat with garlic and oil; serve over rice or spaghetti. This can also work with any leftover chicken or meat cut up.

Hamburger

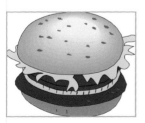

Fry or broil a hamburger or turkey or vegetable patty. Serve either on a bun or plated with baked potato and green salad.

Brown hamburger or ground turkey in a large fry pan; add jar or canned tomato sauce; serve over spaghetti or macaroni or rice.

Hot Dogs

Brown hot dogs or kielbasa; serve on rolls or cut up into baked beans. (Vegetarian baked beans taste really good and have less fat in them.)

Baked potatoes

Wash potato well, pierce it with a fork, place in hot oven (425 degrees) and bake for about 45 minutes. Or pierce the potato with a fork, then microwave for about 10 minutes; then continue baking in the oven at 425 degrees until done (soft to the squeeze) or cut in half then, and finish cooking by placing cut-side down into oiled fry pan and cook over medium heat.

Served topped with vegetables, cheese and/or bacon bits, they can be a meal by themselves.

Slow cooked meat

Buy a cheap cut of beef roast. Put it in a slow cooker or a large heavy pot over low heat; add two small cans of beef broth; cook for 6 hours in the slow cooker or about two hours on the stove. You can shred the beef to use for tacos or burritos or for sandwiches or other leftover meals; you can also add vegetables and use one can of beef broth and one can of tomato soup and make it a stew. You can do this with chicken too.

Roast Chicken

Roast a chicken or buy one already roasted from the store. If you roast a chicken or turkey, always remove the wrapped gizzard from inside the bird.

Slice the breast meat for sandwiches; pick all the rest of the chicken from the bones and you can use that meat for chicken salad (add mayo, chopped celery, salt and pepper) or add to spaghetti sauce over noodles or add to an omelet or baked potato...etc.

Biscuits

Biscuits can be made easily with Bisquick OR you can try Michael's Mom's favorite easy recipe:

Mix together 2 cups flour, 2 Tablespoons of sugar, 4 teaspoons of baking powder, ½ teaspoon of salt. Add ½ cup canola oil, 1 slightly beaten egg and 2/3 cup of milk. Stir together to make a soft dough (don't overmix it). Drop by large tablespoons onto an ungreased cookie sheet and bake for 10-12 minutes in a hot oven at 450 degrees.

Kathy says to remind you not to "overwork" the dough. Too much stirring and kneading will make the biscuits heavy. (Her son called them hockey pucks.)

Leftover biscuits are great heated up or toasted in toaster. Spread with jelly...YUM.

French dressing

Blend together a can of tomato soup, 1 cup sugar, 1 cup vinegar, 1 cup salad oil, 1 small finely chopped onion, 1 teaspoon dry mustard, and a dash of hot sauce. Store in refrigerator.

Green Salad

Buy already packaged salad OR, for more economical salad, buy lettuce by the head, carrots, red cabbage, radishes, broccoli, cauliflower, jicama, tomatoes, and any other vegetable you like. Rinse lettuce under cold water and dry on paper towels. Rinse under cold water, peel, grate, and/or chop all the other vegetables. Keep tomatoes separate if you are not going to eat the salad completely at one sitting (it spoils the lettuce quickly if you put them together).

Stuffed vegetables

Brown ground meat (beef, pork, chicken or turkey); add cooked white rice (can add cottage cheese); use to stuff cabbage leaves, green or red peppers, zucchini, tomatoes, etc.

Top with parmesan cheese and bake at 350 degrees for 20-40 minutes.

Meatloaf or meatballs

Add about ¼ cup bread crumbs and one raw egg to 1 pound of ground beef or turkey; add garlic, salt and pepper; mix well... you can make this into meat balls to cook in tomato sauce or bake in the oven and then add to tomato sauce, or bake as a meatloaf, or brown as hamburger patties.

"LEFTOVER" MEALS:

Leftover chicken cut-up into cream of mushroom soup can be served over rice or toast.

Leftover meat browned with taco seasoning and re-fried beans can be rolled up in tortillas.

Meat turnovers

Grind up leftover meat; make biscuit dough (from previous page); spread some flour on a clean cutting board; on the board, pat dough into small circles; place ground meat in center and fold to make a turnover; bake at 450 for about 15 minutes. Serve with packaged gravy or heated up stewed tomatoes.

Cut up leftover beef or chicken

Mix with veggies of your choice; add cream of mushroom or golden mushroom soup; cook on stove top. This can be served over rice or with biscuits or top with dumplings made from biscuit dough and cook for 20 minutes covered and then 20 minutes uncovered.

QUICK DESSERTS

Keep **frozen cookie dough** on hand to make quick treats. Warm cookies are better—and cheaper—than the packaged kind.

Fruit turnovers are easy: Make biscuits like for the meat turnovers, but instead of meat in the center, add cut-up cooking apples (such as Granny Smith, Pippin, or Macintosh). Sprinkle with cinnamon and bake the same way. You can also do this with ready-made pie dough that you find with the refrigerator biscuits in the store.

Cake mixes are great to have on hand and can be easily frozen unfrosted to keep for a long time. Instead of frosting, add canned fruit with Cool Whip.

Tip: Either freeze pieces of cake already cut-up or freeze as a whole (without frosting). You will be able to cut off a piece even though it is frozen. Pop it in the microwave for about ½ minute and it's ready to eat. (you can also put a slice in a toaster or toaster oven) Add a scoop of ice cream or some canned fruit, and you have dessert.

If you want to frost your cake, Linda has just the trick: her Grandma Emma's Never Fail Frosting. She says "This is better than the kind you can buy, and much less expensive. And it's easy."

Blend in a saucepan: ½ cup sugar, 1 Tablespoon cornstarch; then add ¼ cup milk and 2 Tablespoons butter or margarine. Heat in a saucepan until it boils, stirring as it cooks (about 5 minutes); let it cool and stir in about 2 cups of confectioner's (powdered) sugar until it's smooth and the right consistency to spread. If it's too thick, add a little milk; if it's too thin, add more powdered sugar.

There are lots of variations: Add 1 block of baker's chocolate or ¼ cup baking cocoa for chocolate icing. Blend in ¼ cup peanut butter with the chocolate for my son's favorite icing (especially on a chocolate cake). Use brown sugar instead of white in the original mix for a special icing

Fruit makes a great dessert. Remember to rinse fresh fruit well before you use it— but don't wash it until you are ready to use it or it will spoil faster. If you want fruit to ripen quickly, put it in a paper bag. Once it's ripe, keep it in the refrigerator.

Fresh fruit can be cut up into a salad. OR fresh strawberries can be cut ahead of time, sprinkled with a little sugar and mashed up a bit with a fork. Left overnight or for a few hours and they will have a juice to make your strawberry shortcake yummy.

Canned fruit can be spooned over ice cream or plain cake or biscuits. Add cool whip to make it a special treat. Get canned fruit without added sugar if possible.

Food Preparation Tips

• Put together enough salad for a couple of days; store in a zip-lock bag, squeezing out excess air.

• Keep **bananas** in a cool place and in a sealed plastic bag to make them last longer. Also break them apart; bananas hooked together at the stems will spoil quicker. Bananas can be peeled and frozen to use later in banana bread or in smoothies.

• Store **leftover food** in meal-sized containers or freezer bags in the freezer and **mark** with the date and contents.

• **Scrub carrots** instead of peeling them.

• **Wash lettuce** in cold water, then wrap in paper towels to store in the refrigerator.

• **Cut onions** from the **top**, not starting where the roots come out, and they will stay fresh longer and make your eyes tear up less. Cold onions cause less tearing too.

• Don't refrigerate fresh **garlic**. Keep it in a cool dry place, not in an air tight package.

• When boiling an **egg**, add salt to the water to make it easier to peel. Also put a pin hole in the blunt end of the egg to avoid having the shell crack. If it is still giving you trouble in shelling it, run it under cold water while you are peeling it.

• The deeper the color of fruit and vegetables, the more nutritious it is.

- Before baking or cooking something by a **recipe**, put all the ingredients on the counter to make sure you have everything. Put the ingredients away as you use them and you won't have to wonder if you remembered to add everything—and your clean-up will be easier.

- At the end of cooking a meal, fill the largest dirty pan with water and soap and let dishes **soak** in it while you eat.

- Always keep scissors where you can reach them quickly.

- Don't put sharp **knives** in the dishwasher; their blades get dull.

- Freeze chicken or beef **broth** in ice cube trays, then put in freezer bag. You'll have them on-hand to add to recipes in small measures.

- Shredded **cheese** can be frozen to have on hand for quick meals.

- Always **freeze** in quantities that you can thaw quickly and use in that amount. Remember that things freeze together and may be difficult to separate, such as hot dogs.

- You can freeze **bread** in packets of three or four slices so that it doesn't go moldy, especially in the summer. Just remove and set on counter to thaw before using. Keeping your bread in the refrigerator will keep it from going moldy too.

- When **whipping** egg whites or whipped cream, put the beaters and the bowl in the freezer to get cold before starting. Make sure there are no bits of yolk or blood in the egg white or it won't whip up.

Substitution tips

If you run out of something, there are often substitutes that may be used, such as:

Use butter, margarine or shortening as replacements for each other.

Applesauce may be substituted for shortening or oil in some baked items.

Baking soda and lemon juice or soured milk can replace equal amount of baking powder.

Use sharper cheese in recipes because you need less of it to get full flavor.

Softer cheese melts better than hard cheese.

Equivalent weights & measures in cooking:

1 dash = 8 drops of liquid

1 cup = 16 tablespoons

1 tablespoon = 3 teaspoons

4 tablespoons = ¼ cup

8 tablespoons = ½ cup

16 tablespoons = 1 cup

4 cups = 1 quart

4 quarts = 1 gallon

28 saltine crackers = 1 cup of cracker crumbs

4 slices of toasted/dried bread = 1 cup of bread crumbs

1 stick of butter = 1/2 cup

1 liter of liquid = 1.06 quart

CLEANING

STOCKING CLEANING SUPPLIES

Broom and dustpan

Sponges – at least three: one for floors, one for dishes, one for cleaning. Mark each with indelible marker so you can identify which is for what

Scrubber such as Brillo

Old **towels** or rags

Plastic **bucket** and mop

Cleanser such as Comet or Ajax

Liquid all-purpose cleaner such as 409 or Pinesol

Window cleaner such as Windex

Old **toothbrush**

Laundry detergent

Dish **detergent**

Paper towels

White vinegar

Ammonia

3% hydrogen peroxide

Tip: Play some music you enjoy, something peppy, when you're cleaning. It will make the jobs seem quicker and easier.

CLEANING ROUTINES AND TIPS

Daily.......................

- Make the **bed** every day – it sets the tone for your day.

- Manage **clutter** – whenever you leave a room, take a quick look around and straighten up anything that is out of place – the key to a neat home is to keep at it all the time. Don't let chores or clutter pile-up.

- Sort your **mail** – take the time to look through everything as you bring it in. Don't let mail pile up; bills may get lost in the shuffle. Sort it near a trash can and rip up anything you don't keep. Cut up credit cards into slivers with scissors.

- **Clean** as you cook – it keeps the **kitchen** cleaner and healthier.

- **Wipe up spills** immediately – cleaning is always quicker and easier if done right away..

- **Sweep** the kitchen floor – make it the last thing you do after dinner and clean-up.

Weekly.......................

Kitchen

* Wipe inside **oven** and **microwave**

* Discard foods and beverages from **refrigerator**

* Flush **drain** with boiling water

* Wipe **surfaces**

* Clean **trash** bin

* Vacuum and mop **floor**

Living Room

* Fluff and rotate **couch** cushions

* Discard **magazines** and clutter

* **Dust**

* **Vacuum**

Home Office or area where you keep your bills

- Sort through **mail** and accumulated **papers**

- Pay bills and file them

- Dust / empty trash / vacuum

Bedroom

* **Strip** off the sheets to wash

* **Open windows,** if possible, to air the room

(note: sunshine and fresh air keeps your home from smelling damp.)

* Discard magazines or **clutter**

* **Dust** / empty **trash** /

* Make up bed with **clean sheets**

* Shake out small **rugs** / **vacuum** / **sweep** floor

Tip: If you spend a couple of minutes each day to keep your closet and drawers straightened out , you won't have a giant job waiting for you on a weekly or monthly basis. And it is so nice to be able to find things.

Bathroom

* Clean toilet, **bathtub,** shower, and **sink** .

* Wipe mirrors

* Change and launder **bath mats** and towels & **washcloths**

* Dust light fixtures

* Empty **trash**

* Vacuum and mop floor

Throughout the house

* Launder machine washable **throw rugs**

* Wipe hand-prints and pet prints from

 windows, doors, and walls

* Vacuum and mop **floors**

Monthly...........in addition to "weekly"

Kitchen

* Wash ventilation hood **filters** over stove

* Discard food in freezer and de-ice if necessary

* Straighten out **cupboards** or pantry

Living Room

* Vacuum rugs

* Clean **fireplace**, if you have one. (Make sure there are no hot coals.)

Bedroom

* Launder mattress pads, shams, coverlets

Bathroom

* Scrub **tub** (and grout); spray with mold killer

* Wipe insides of medicine cabinet

Closets

* **Dust** shelves and storage bins

* Wipe baseboards

* Vacuum or sweep **floors**

Throughout the house

* Vacuum window tracks and screens

* Dust **ceiling fans**

* Wipe doors, light switch plates, & telephones

* **Flush drains** with vinegar, boiling water & baking soda

* Polish furniture

* Clean **mirrors**

Seasonally..................

Kitchen

* **Replace box of baking soda** in refrigerator and freezer (baking soda absorbs odors)

* Clean oven

* Wipe inside of **refrigerator**

Cleaning Tips

Bedroom

* Turn mattress over and vacuum it

* Launder **pillows**

NEVER mix ammonia with any other detergent or cleanser – it gives off poisonous fumes.

> To clean an oven:

Heat the oven; then turn it **off**. Place a small bowl of **ammonia** in the oven and **close** the door. Leave **overnight**. In the morning, grease will be runny and can be **wiped off.**

To **clean deep stain in a porcelain sink**:

Line the sink with paper towels and carefully pour some bleach to wet the towels. Leave sit overnight. Scrub with cleanser the next day.

Be careful of cleansers with bleach, such as Tilex.

They can bleach your clothing or towels by accident.

To get **melted wax** out of carpeting, layer paper towels over the wax and apply heat with a hair dryer. Blot the spot to absorb the wax.

Fold clothes as soon as they are done drying or wrinkles will set in.

Trick:
There are common items that will do a lot of things around the house for less money than the fancy packaged and advertised products.

Hydrogen peroxide

Hydrogen peroxide is one of those items. Most homes have a brown bottle of 3% hydrogen peroxide somewhere in their bathroom. If not, you can buy it very cheaply in grocery stores, drugstores, and places like Walmart and Target. The most common use for peroxide is to **clean cuts and treat infections**. If you have a cut, dab it with peroxide on a cotton ball or pour a little peroxide right over the injury. It will fizzle up, lifting those germs right out of your wound. But its uses don't end there.

Hint: Karen, a nurse for more years than she's telling, swears by hydrogen peroxide to take blood out of washable cloth. Just pour some on the stain while holding the item over the sink. If it is a big stain or an old stain, you may need to leave the item in the sink with peroxide covering the stain. Then just wring it out and toss it in the wash. If you cannot get the item in a sink, try dabbing it with a little peroxide on a cotton ball.

Peroxide can be used as a **mouthwash** and it is much cheaper and more effective than the usual rinses. Just fill the cap from the bottle with peroxide, then pour it into your mouth, holding it there for up to 10 minutes before spitting it out. Your teeth will be whiter and you will have no more canker sores and less gum problems. You can even do it while you take a shower.

Do not worry about swallowing the peroxide; it will not hurt you. It is also good to help lessen the pain of a **toothache** until you can get to a dentist. Just hold a capful of peroxide in your mouth over the sore tooth several times a day.

You can soak your **toothbrush** in a glass with enough peroxide in it to cover the bristles, keeping your toothbrush germ-free. Use some on a cleaning cloth to wipe down your sink and counter too.

WD-40

Another common item you can usually find in most households is a can of **WD-40**. You can buy this in hardware stores, Target and Walmart, and grocery and drug stores. This amazing spray is a lubricant extraordinaire (the WD stands for water displacement).

Charlotte says: *Here's a list of possibilities for using WD-40, but you'll think up even more once you get the idea:*

* Removes road tar and grime from cars

* Cleans and lubricates guitar strings

* Removes lipstick stains from clothing

* Loosens stubborn zippers

* Helps to untangle jewelry chains

* Removes dirt and grime from barbecue grills

* Removes stains from stainless steel sinks

* Keeps ceramic/terra cotta garden pots from getting white residue on the outside (called oxidizing)

* Camouflages scratches in ceramic and marble floors

* Keeps scissors working smoothly

* Takes the "squeak" out of noisy door hinges on doors in homes and vehicles

* Removes black scuff marks on floors

*Takes bug guts off your car without leaving marks (use a soft cloth to wipe)

* Restores and cleans leather dashboards

* Rids rocking chairs and electric fans of squeaks

 * Makes windows and closet doors slide smoothly and quietly

* Keeps rust from forming on saws and garden tools

* Removes grease on stoves and traces of tape

* Keeps pigeons off balconies (they don't like the smell)

* Removes crayon marks from walls

Laundry softening sheets (like Bounce) can deodorize your shoes and sneakers. Just put a sheet in each shoe overnight.

You can also put sheets in your dresser drawers, your laundry basket, your car, or your wastebasket.

Checking online, we found that other uses like keeping away ants or bees or mosquitoes were reportedly untrue. But you can try that yourself and see.

DOING THE LAUNDRY

If you don't have a job that gets your clothes really dirty, buy the cheaper detergent. However, if you need to get heavy dirt out, a more expensive detergent like Tide may be necessary.

Always read the washing directions on clothing tags before washing.

The Basics of Laundry

Sort by color and type:

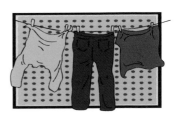

> whites and light colors together

> towels of any color together

> dark clothes together (turn black pants inside out to keep them black longer)

> you may need to separate anything that may be fuzzy or permanent press into a different load

> hand wash delicate things separately (sweaters, silky blouses, etc.) with Woolite. (Don't use too much.)

Trick: Use large safety pins to keep socks together in the wash.

Wash **whites** and **towels** with **warm** water; **colors** with cold.

Put the **soap** into the water to **dissolve** fully BEFORE you put the clothes in. If soap gets directly onto your clothes, you may have spots of soap on them when you're done. Then you need to rewash.

Do not put **delicate things** like panties and bras or spandex things in the **dryer**. Heat will affect the elastic and turn synthetic cloth a dingy grey.

Dry for the **shortest time** necessary. Dryers use a lot of electricity which means higher bills!

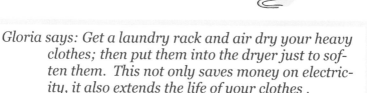

Gloria says: Get a laundry rack and air dry your heavy clothes; then put them into the dryer just to soften them. This not only saves money on electricity, it also extends the life of your clothes .

Important: Always clean the **lint trap** on your dryer for every use! You should wash it in hot water once in a while if you use fabric softener (it sticks to the screen and cuts the air flow). Also check the **vent** yearly. Clogged lint traps and vents can cut down on the effectiveness of your dryer, costing you more money; and they can cause **fires**.

Laundry tips

Pre-treat stains before washing garments.

Do not dry in dryer before you are sure the stain is gone as heat will "set" it and make removal impossible.

Stain removal sticks are good to have on hand.

Hydrogen peroxide removes **blood** stains.

Fold your laundry while watching a favorite television show; it makes it go faster.

Check the **amount of detergent** that is recommended; frequently manufacturers will include large scoops that only need to be half-filled to be sufficient. If you don't pay attention, you'll use up your supply twice as fast as necessary.

Zip any zippers before putting clothes in the washer; they are less likely to break and need replacement.

Lauren says: *If you take clothes out of the dryer as soon as they are dry and hang them up or fold them smoothly, they are less likely to need ironing. If ironing is necessary, take the clothes out while still slightly damp or sprinkle them with water by shaking wet fingers over them, rolling them up and waiting a bit before ironing. You can also put a wrinkled shirt into the dryer for a few minutes to get the wrinkles out. But don't put too many in at a time or for too long.*

Always set the **iron temperature** for the appropriate fabric type (see label). Some are very sensitive to high temperatures. Test the heat on an inside hem or someplace you can't see if you're not sure. Stretch seams a bit while you iron over them so they don't pucker. Irons use a lot of electricity to heat up, so don't iron just one piece at a time. If possible, do all your ironing for the week at one time to save electricity and money.

Trick: Keep a small jar near the dryer to save any loose change you find in the machines. Kate says she would treat her son Michael to a banana split when there was enough change in the jar.

THOUGHT FOR THE DAY:

Live the motto of "Use it up, wear it out, fix it up, make do" before replacing something.

LIVING LIGHTLY

Linda says: *Living lightly means to conserve our natural world as much as possible, such as using less electricity and protecting the environment.*

- **Buying quality** items may be economical in the long term.

- **Turn off lights and appliances** when they are not being used. This applies to things like chargers; if you see any kind of light on, it's using electricity.

- Use **cloth bags** for grocery shopping.

- Replace regular light bulbs with **compact fluorescent lights**; they may cost more to buy but will last much longer and lower your electric bill.

- **Dry clothes on a line** or a rack whenever possible. Save the dryer for fluffing only or for rainy days.

- **Keep freezers full**. Full freezers use less electricity so keep bags of ice in your freezer if you need to take up space.

- **Re-use plastic water bottles**, filling them from the tap. You can also fill half-full and freeze; then fill with water before leaving the house, keeping the water cold for a long time.

- To **wash fruit and vegetables**, fill two spray bottles: one with hydrogen peroxide and one with white vinegar. Spray fruits and vegetables with both and rinse with tap water.

RECYCLE & REUSE

- **Don't let water run** while you wash dishes, brush your teeth or shave.

- **Recycle everything, all the time**.

GETTING ALONG WITH OTHERS

SELF ESTEEM AND ATTITUDE

Only YOU can change your attitude and self image. Do not expect others to "make" you feel good about yourself.

Take charge of yourself!

Start by:

• Smiling. Just the act of smiling can increase your good mood and reach out in a positive manner to others. Try answering the phone with a smile, and you'll notice the difference in your tone of voice.

• Look your best at all times. Find someone you respect and admire, then fashion yourself in that image.

• Get a good night's sleep.

• Keep positive thoughts about yourself and break any pattern of negative self-talk.

• Keep your car clean, inside and out. It reflects your own self-image.

• Play happy music with upbeat lyrics. Even if you are not consciously listening to it, the music will react on your subconscious.

• Walk with your head up and your shoulders squared. Like a smile, an erect posture works to put a positive spin on your attitude on a subconscious level.

> **Sandra sends this advice:** *TRUTH is a very important behavior to learn and practice. Does what you say create friendships? Is it beneficial to both people? Have you really listened to what they said? Life is nothing more than talking and listening. Remember to: L T W T S — Listen To What They Say.*

SETTING UP YOUR OWN RULES

There are critical events in our lives that we have to manage without the counsel or support of parents or others upon whom we have depended in the past. We may have decided not to call upon previous resources or we may have none who we trust. We need to develop more interpersonal skills, resolve conflict, or avoid some relationships.

In order to successfully navigate these challenges, each individual needs guidelines—

a personal set of rules to live by.

You may find help to do this in books: such as Covey's **7 habits of highly successful individuals**. Read any book carefully before deciding what parts you agree with and want to keep, and what parts you do not. Put your rules in writing so you can refer back to them—and they are more real when they have been written down.

Another strategy is to choose a **role model**—someone who you admire—and try to make decisions that you think he or she would approve. This is something like "What would Jesus do?" or "What would Martin Luther King do?" or perhaps "What would Hillary Clinton do?" Or you might choose someone close to you who you believe has made a success of his or her life. Study that person and learn what you can about how they handle situations, what "rules" for life they follow.

Kate tell us that she wears a beaded bracelet that has the letters "WWJD" on it. It reminds her to think about what she does during the day, hopefully remembering to model her actions after the examples of how Jesus lived.

> **Tip**: This can also be used to help handle people who are pestering you to do something you are not comfortable with. Just tell them that it (whatever "it" is) is against **your** rules.

Regardless of how you do it, you must construct a set of personal guidelines—<u>your</u> rules. You may choose to include some of the rules you were raised with, but they are still "your" rules because have chosen them independently.

Your rules to live by may include things like not drinking or doing drugs, safe sex, eating healthy, turning away from conflict, refusing to do violence, being on time every day for work, paying your bills on time, going to church... these are the behaviors and values that will shape your life as you go, and you will find you need to fine-tune them as you grow.

EMPLOYMENT

FINDING A JOB

• Keep a positive attitude about yourself and your own worth without being cocky.

• If you are using a resume, make sure that it is neat and clean and free of any errors. Have someone else check it for you, even if you are sure it is perfect.

• When you meet a prospective employer, look them in the eye, smile, shake hands firmly, and keep your posture up.

• Make sure you are dressed appropriately in clean, neat clothes. Dressing for success means wearing clothes to an interview that you would be expected to wear in the position you want to obtain. Always dress up, never down. Do not dress sexy.

• Keep jewelry to a minimum.

• Cover tattoos if possible.

• Be on time for any meeting.

• Libraries usually will have access to Internet for job searches. Newspapers are also leads.

• You can also do "cold calls" with a phone book, calling or dropping in on companies/businesses where you would like to work. If you do drop in, be dressed for a meeting and be armed with your resume.

> **Ask people you know if they would be references for you. Usually the best choices for references are people already in the field that you are interested in. They will need to be able to say that you are qualified, that you are a good worker, and that you can be trusted.**

PRESENTING A GOOD
IMAGE FOR WORK

To keep your job, and to move up in position, you need to walk the walk all the time. The advice given in previous pages about how to obtain a job is the same for keeping a job.

• Look around at the other workers (the successful ones) to gauge what are appropriate clothes, appropriate behavior and language, minimal jewelry, punctuality.

• Be respectful of others; use "Sir" or "Ma'm" in talking to those in positions above you.

• Be punctual.

• Be trustworthy.

• Do not gossip or use street language or tell graphic jokes.

• If you don't know how to do something, admit it and ask for help.

• Thank people who help you--always.

INTERVIEW TIPS

When you interview for a job, the interviewer wants to find out:

1. if you are **qualified** for the position

2. if you are **motivated** to do the job

3. if you are the **right person** to fit with others

How can you improve your chances for being hired? Here are tips that experienced interviewers recommend....

First: Treat every job prospect with respect and present yourself as if the job, no matter what it is, is important. So act as if the job for which you are applying is actually a higher-up position than it is.

Preparation will help you remain calm during the interview:

Research the company through the Internet or the library to learn relevant facts such as what they do and locations.

Look your best. Wear neutral colors.

Organize the night before. Your interview clothing and resume should all be ready to go. Get a good night's rest.

Give yourself plenty of **time** to get there.

Know the **exact place and time** of the meeting, the interviewer's full name (including correct pronunciation), and his or her title.

Dos ...

• Arrive on time or a few minutes early.

• Greet your interviewer with a firm handshake and an enthusiastic smile.

• If presented with an application, fill it out neatly and completely. Don't attach a resume unless you're told to do so.

• Call the interviewer by last name if you are sure of the pronunciation. If not, ask the employer to repeat it.

- Wait until you're offered a chair before sitting. Sit upright, look alert and interested at all times.

- Listen carefully and respond in a few words. Look the hiring manager in the eye while speaking.

Don'ts ...

If you don't understand a question - or if you need a moment to think about your answer - say so.
Never pretend to know something or someone when you don't.

Don't inquire about salary, vacations, benefits, bonuses or retirement on the initial interview unless you are sure the employer is interested in hiring you.

??????????????????????????????

Be prepared to answer requests like these :

Tell me about yourself. Vary your response according to the specific job opportunity and offer a brief description of why you would be a good fit for the position. One of the best ways to prepare for an interview is to rehearse and then review your answers.

Tell me about your background, accomplishments, strengths and weaknesses.
Giver a short summary of your experience.

Tell me why I should hire you. Even if you do not have experience in this job, stress how eager you are to learn, what a diligent worker you are, and how your attitude and commitment will make up for any lack of experience. You need to convince them that you **really** want the job.

Prepare some questions you might ask, such as

- What would I be expected to accomplish in this position?

- What are the greatest challenges in this position?

- What kind of person are you looking for to fill this position?

TRANSPORTATION

Buying a car:

Establishing good credit is important if you want to buy a car. Use your credit to make small purchases and pay the bill in FULL every month. You cannot buy a car unless you have cash or credit so you can finance. The only other option is to use a friend or parent as a cosigner.

Tip: "The most important thing for any driver to remember" says Richard (a long time trucker)" is to pay attention to what is going on around you."

Tips for buying a car

Research the vehicle you are interested in on the Internet at Dealership, Car Max, or Auto Trader web sites. Or you can check the newspaper ads.

Rental returns can be a good buy. Hertz, Enterprise and other rental companies also sell their used rental cars.

Check prices at NADA.com, Kelly BB.com, or Edmonds.com.

You can also check J.D. Powers or Consumers Reports.

You can check **vehicle history** at CarFax.com

Consider buying from a reputable new or used car dealer. If you buy from a private party you should have the vehicle checked by a mechanic.

At a car dealership, always ask for the Fleet/Internet Department and not the regular sales force. They give better pricing.

Be careful during the finance phase of the purchase. They may try to sell you a lot of extra "stuff" like alarms, paint protective coatings, security etchings, etc. Generally you do not need any of this or you can get it cheaper elsewhere (like alarm systems).

Warranties are nice, but expensive; they are usually marked up to double their cost. The price on these can be negotiated.

Tip: If you want to protect your seats, buy a couple of spray cans of Scotch-guard or something similar. It will accomplish the same thing as the more expensive protective sprays that dealers sell.

Tip: Never rush into a car deal. If it doesn't feel right, it probably is not a good deal.

Safe Driving

Keep a **safe distance**, loaded trucks can weigh as much as 50,000 pounds while the average car weighs 3,000 pounds. Do not cut off a truck, his stopping distance is much greater than yours. Trucks have a large blind spot; if you can't see the driver's face in his mirror he can't see you. Don't pass a truck on the right side, or tailgate. The driver will have a hard time seeing you. Safe driving and common sense is the key.

Do not allow **distractions** like cell phones, changing channels on radio, looking at directions to take your focus off the traffic. If you need to, pull over and park.

Keep a **cool head** when dealing with other drivers. Everybody makes mistakes; **practice patience**.

Slow down in any kind of bad weather!

Supplies to keep in car:

- **First aid kit**
- **Fire extinguisher**
- **Road flares or triangles**
- **Basic tool kit**
- **Extra fan belt**
- **Spare tire (aired up)**
- **Jack & lug wrench**
- **Cell phone with emergency numbers**
- **Water and a blanket**

Owning a car:

•   Once you own a vehicle, make a **folder** for the paperwork and keep it in a safe place.

•   Keep a record of all **maintenance** and **repairs** done on the car, for your use and for whenever you go to sell it.

•   Establish yourself with a **mechanic/repair** place. Ask around for who is reputable.

•   Keep your car **clean inside and out**. It is a reflection of you as a person and it is as important to keep it presentable as it is to keep yourself presentable.

•   Drive sensibly to protect yourself and to save fuel: slower speeds, no fast starts, combined errands, etc.

TIP

**CHANGE THE OIL REGULARLY.
This is the single most important thing you can do to keep
your car running well and last-
ing long.**

Transportation without owning a car:

•   Check on **bus** lines or **light rail access** when you choose an apartment. Check the bus companies about discounts for buying monthly or yearly passes.

•   Inquire at job interviews if there is **carpooling**.

•   Ask co-workers if they would be interested in **transporting** you to and from work with them if you chip in for gas. Get an agreement up front on how much you will each chip in per week or per day.

PARENTING

Child Care and Discipline

Now it's your turn to do for your child what you wish had been done for you!

Here are some tips that everyone can benefit by, parents or not:

Don't be afraid to say NO.

All children will test for their boundaries and are more comfortable and secure once they know them.

Be consistent in your rules and demands. And once you have made a decision, stick to it.

Never threaten. Never ever call your children names like "stupid" or "dummy."

Treat your child with kindness and love at all times. Let them know you love them without reservation and no matter what they have done.

Be as courteous to your child as you would be to an adult whom you respect. We teach best by example. Never talk down to them.

Practice what you preach. Teaching by example means letting them see you say please and thank you, smile often, laugh and sing, brush your teeth, wash your hands before dinner, etc.

Sit down together for meals as a family and talk, don't lecture them. Meals should be a time of talking and listening pleasantly.

Pay attention to your child.

Attend church together.

Stay in contact with their school and teachers.

Do not discipline them in front of others; if necessary, take them to another room or aside and talk to them in private so you don't embarrass or belittle them.

Teach them to feel good about themselves. Let them know that you are proud of them.

Do not push your child too fast or hang onto them too long. The ability to be independent is the best gift we can give them when they are ready to take the responsibility that comes with it.

Give children chores to do; this teaches them responsibility and helps them have confidence in themselves.

Let them help you in the kitchen and teach them skills for when they become adults

Have fun with them.

They grow up fast.

Options for Moving into a Brighter Future

Looking Ahead

Living independently means accepting the challenges of providing the necessities for your survival—money to live on, a place to live, health coverage.

It also means making decisions about your future.

Your first job may be entry level or manual labor. To move up the economic ladder, you will need to obtain advanced skills.

Here we have included a couple of **options** that our own children or grandchildren or nieces or nephews have taken. Perhaps one of them would be right for you.

Military Service Option

Active duty military service provides an adequate initial salary, provides good housing and extensive quality medical care.

Direct benefits include strong technical training in a wide range of career areas that are normally geared to utilize individual aptitudes, prior experience and service needs.

Indirect benefits include: healthy lifestyles, training and physical fitness regimens, interpersonal relationship training, and an opportunity to travel.

Military service also makes thousands of dollars of **education benefits** possible with the completion of the first term of enlistment.

Military service personnel may **retire** after only 20 years of successful service with a lifetime retirement income and health benefits, which can be the equivalent of hundreds of thousands of dollars. However, long service in the military is dependent upon demonstrating the ability to assume increasing levels of responsibility and leadership, and the ever increasing mastery of increasing levels of technical skills.

The down-side of military service for most individuals is the possibility of facing life-threatening combat situations. **Note**: While service in any of the military branches can place the members in combat situations, the Air Force, Navy, and Coast Guard present the **lowest risk** based on the types and locations of operations; the Army and Marines are the highest risk. The career area you choose also has a strong influence on the possibility of getting into conflict.

ATTENTION !!!!!

Normally, active military service requires a **two to three** year commitment. Enlistees have to successfully complete the basic training, after which each member goes through initial technical training in a specific area. The member then moves to their first service station. Military members are stationed all around the world.

Military service can provide not only the fundamental necessities for independent living and outstanding educational benefits, it can also provide a very solid platform for a successful life.

Military service is also widely respected by most citizens in the United States and many businesses recognize the beneficial things that service provides to the members: training, leadership, responsibility.

AmeriCorps Option

AmeriCorps is the umbrella program name for a family of community service programs sponsored by the federal government. Some of these programs, specifically the AmeriCorps National Civilian Community Corps (NCCC), and some AmeriCorps State programs can provide the basic necessities required for transition from foster care to independent living.

Unlike military service, which provides a reasonable initial salary, comfortable housing, and total health coverage, residential AmeriCorps programs offer only a small living stipend, rudimentary housing, and a limited health benefit sufficient to cover the basic necessities. However:

AmeriCorps programs have terms of service that vary from 10 to 12 months.

A direct benefit of the AmeriCorps programs is an end-of-term Education Benefit of $4,725 for future education or qualified technical training.

One of the main programs that offer opportunities for transition out of the foster care system is the Ameri-Corps*National Civilian Community Corps. The NCCC is a 10 month, full-time, team based residential community service program.

The NCCC consists of three regional campuses based in Sacramento, California; Denver, Colorado; and Perry Point, Maryland.

Those selected to serve are sent to one of the three campuses at the start of each 10-month class. Sacramento's class currently begins in late summer to early fall, and the other two start in mid-winter (January).

Selectees travel to the assigned campus at the beginning of their term at government expense. Once on campus, the members are assigned to a coed team of 10-12 members plus a Team Leader. Members serve with their initial team for the full term.

After four weeks of initial training, which includes **team building, diversity awareness, CPR, first aid, and Red Cross disaster services,** members embark on nine months of rotational community service projects across the nation.

The range of potential community service projects covers everything that volunteers do in a community: **tutoring/ mentoring in classrooms; working in food banks; building/repairing low income housing; building trails or restoring environmental habitats, and more.** The teams travel to and live in the community where each project is to be completed.

Projects normally last 6 to 8 weeks. Teams are housed in a variety of **housing situations**, depending upon what the project sponsor can provide, which may include anything from individual rooms to tents. Food or a food allowance is provided and teams often get by with cooking team-based community meals. Normally, members see a wide variety of projects during their term of service. Members are also certified in all aspects of Red Cross Disaster Services. During their term, they may be deployed anywhere in the United States in support of a disaster response to provide family services, shelter operations, or logistics.

An indirect benefit of service in AmeriCorps*NCCC is a tremendous immersion in interpersonal relationships and getting along with others.

Unlike a regular job, the members of the team are pretty much together 24/7, having to both work together during the day, and living together in off duty hours.

AmeriCorps*NCCC does not provide in-depth training in any specific career area, but it does give a wide range of training specific to the projects that each team completes.

AmeriCorps*State programs that provide the necessities of transition (income, housing, health coverage) are limited and do not exist in all states.

The majority of programs that do provide these necessities fall into the category of **State Conservation Corps**. The major differences between the State Conservation Corps and the AmeriCorps*NCCC previously discussed are that the state programs normally do not travel outside the state they are located in, and they focus on a single area of community service, normally environmental work.

There are other AmeriCorps programs that offer a variation of options.

All AmeriCorps programs provide some level of stipend, medical benefits, and the end of term Education Award.

To find out more information about all AmeriCorps programs and to find a program that offers the aspects that meet you needs, you can go to: www.AmeriCorps.gov to obtain more information. On the website, you can research the different types of programs and benefits and find one that suits you. You can also apply online for any of the programs.

EDUCATION OPPORTUNITIES

If you want to go somewhere, you first need to know where you are---then you stand a chance. Don't kid yourself.

If you're not where you want to be,

it's up to you to get there.

Set your priorities and WRITE THEM DOWN.

Here's a checklist of questions for you to answer:

Did you graduate from high school?

If not, do you want a diploma?

What kind of job interests you now?

What do you think you'd like to do later?

Do you know where to get help?

If college is something you want,

you can do it.

Here are some things you need to think about:

1. **Not everyone needs to go to college.** Many people make a good living without a college degree. However, on the average, college graduates tend to make more than non-college graduates. If you don't know what you want, the best way to explore your options is probably to speak to a counselor in a local college.

2. **Colleges tend to have very good career counseling offices that every student can use. Sign up for one class—anything—then use the career center at that college.** You can find handouts there that will list all kinds of careers available, what they pay, and what you need to learn to prepare for them. But the best help to you will be the real live people with experience.

There are two main types of college:

Community college or "junior college" (like Sacramento City College)

These offer 2-year degrees in many fields which can lead directly to jobs.

They also offer the first two years of 4- or 5-year programs; you transfer to a 4 year college to get a "bachelor's" degree (BA or BS). They are relatively inexpensive.

Four year college (like Sacramento State) or
Universities (like U. C. Davis)

These are for people who have done well in high school,
and who are ready for higher level work right away.
These schools are generally quite a bit more expensive
than community colleges, but there may be scholarship
money available.

**TIP: The best and most useful classes you will
ever take are English classes.**

**Learning to read and write well will help you in
every phase of life.**

**Whether it is a car repair manual, a computer re-
pair or service bulletin, or a college class, you will
need to be able to read and understand.**

**And in almost any job, you will need to be able to
write in a way that can be understood by others.**

**This cannot be stressed enough. Reading
and writing are essential building blocks for
your life.**

Emergency Contacts

Useful Contacts

Finding Help